To
from
GUESS WHO?

SECRET SANTA
COLORING CARD

the best
time
of the
year

Believe
IN THE
Magic
OF
Christmas

it's CHRiSTMAS TiME

Jingle
all
the way

"Santa is watching"

oh
what
fun

Warm Wishes

Oh holy night!

Sparkle all the way

let it
snow

merry
Shine
bright

it's the most
wonderful
time
of
the year

Feliz
Navidad

Merry
Christmas
Happy
New
Year!

enjoy
your
holiday